Milton HERSHEY

by Sarah L. Schuette

Consulting Editor: Gail Saunders-Smith, PhD

Consultant: Pamela Whitenack
Director, Hershey Community Archives
Hershey, Pennsylvania

CAPSTONE PRESS
a capstone imprint

Pebble Books are published by Capstone Press,
1710 Roe Crest Drive, North Mankato, Minnesota 56003
www.capstonepub.com

Library of Congress Cataloging-in-Publication Data
Schuette, Sarah L., 1976–
Milton Hershey / by Sarah L. Schuette.
pages cm. — (Pebble. Business leaders.)
Includes bibliographical references and index.
Summary: "Simple text and photographs present the life of Milton Hershey, founder of the
Hershey Company"—Provided by publisher.
Audience: Grades K to 3.
ISBN 978-1-4765-9640-2 (library binding)
ISBN 978-1-4765-9644-0 (paperback)
ISBN 978-1-4765-9648-8 (eBook PDF)
1. Hershey, Milton Snavely, 1857–1945—Juvenile literature. 2. Businesspeople—United States—
Biography—Juvenile literature. 3. Hershey Foods Corporation—History—Juvenile literature. 4.
Chocolate industry—United States—History—Juvenile literature. 5. Candy industry—United
States—History—Juvenile literature. I. Title.
HD9200.U52H4762 2014
338.7'66392092—dc23
[B]   2013035613

Note to Parents and Teachers

The Business Leaders set supports national social studies standards
related to people, places, and environments. This book describes
and illustrates Milton Hershey. The images support early readers in
understanding the text. The repetition of words and phrases helps
early readers learn new words. This book also introduces early
readers to subject-specific vocabulary words, which are defined
in the Glossary section. Early readers may need assistance to read
some words and to use the Table of Contents, Glossary, Read More,
Internet Sites, and Index sections of the book.

Printed in the United States of America in North Mankato, Minnesota.
092013   007764CGS14

Table of Contents

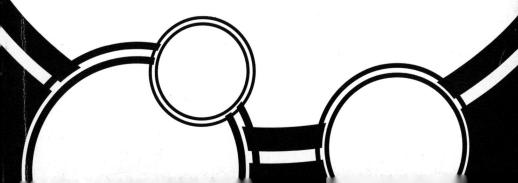

Milton at age 7

1857

born in
Pennsylvania

Early Years

Famous chocolate maker Milton Snavely Hershey was born September 13, 1857, in Pennsylvania. Milton did not get to finish school. He had to start working at a young age.

Milton in 1872

1857

born in
Pennsylvania

1872

apprentice to
candy maker

In 1872 Milton worked as an apprentice to a candy maker. At age 18 Milton opened a candy shop in Philadelphia. It closed in 1882. Milton moved to Lancaster, Pennsylvania, in 1886.

Milton and Kitty in 1910

1857
born in
Pennsylvania

1872
apprentice to
candy maker

1894
starts Hershey
Chocolate Company

Making Chocolate

In 1894 Milton started the Hershey Chocolate Company. Three years later Milton bought the farm in Pennsylvania where he was born. In 1898 Milton married Catherine "Kitty" Sweeney.

1898
marries Catherine "Kitty" Sweeney

10

1857
born in
Pennsylvania

1872
apprentice to
candy maker

1894
starts Hershey
Chocolate Company

In 1900 Milton's company created the Hershey chocolate bar. It was very popular. In 1905 Milton opened a new chocolate factory. Milton and Kitty lived in a house nearby called High Point.

1898 marries Catherine "Kitty" Sweeney

1905 opens chocolate factory

Hershey, Pennsylvania, around 1920

12

1857
born in
Pennsylvania

1872
apprentice to
candy maker

1894
starts Hershey
Chocolate Company

Hershey, Pennsylvania

Milton wanted to help take care of his factory workers. He built them homes too. The town grew. It had schools, stores, a park, and a zoo. The town was named Hershey, Pennsylvania.

1898 — marries Catherine "Kitty" Sweeney

1905 — opens chocolate factory

Pool at Hershey Park, Hershey, Pa. ne of the Hershey Chocolate Co."

1857
born in
Pennsylvania

1872
apprentice to
candy maker

1894
starts Hershey
Chocolate Company

In 1909 Milton started a school for boys in Hershey, Pennsylvania. Education was important to Milton. By the 1930s the town also had an amusement park, hotel, and sports arena.

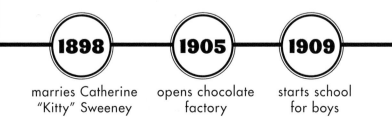

1898
marries Catherine "Kitty" Sweeney

1905
opens chocolate factory

1909
starts school for boys

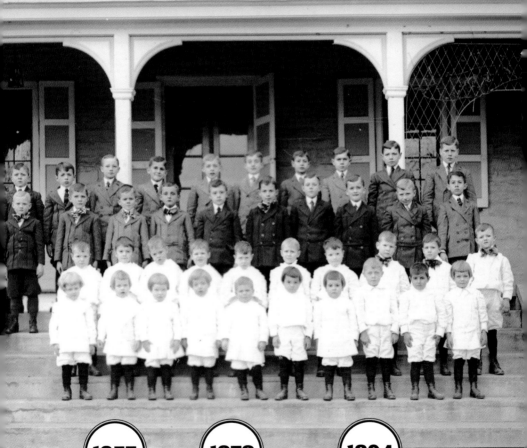

THE HERSHEY INDUSTRIAL SCHOOL.

1857
born in
Pennsylvania

1872
apprentice to
candy maker

1894
starts Hershey
Chocolate Company

Later Years

Milton and Kitty traveled the world. Kitty died in 1915. A few years later, Milton gave his money to the school he and Kitty started together. Taking care of others was important to Milton.

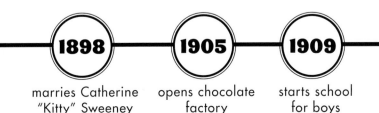

1898
marries Catherine "Kitty" Sweeney

1905
opens chocolate factory

1909
starts school for boys

Hershey bars made
for soldiers

During World War II (1939–1945), Milton's company invented a chocolate bar that didn't melt in hot weather. Eating the bars would give the soldiers energy.

1898
marries Catherine "Kitty" Sweeney

1905
opens chocolate factory

1909
starts school for boys

19

1857
born in
Pennsylvania

1872
apprentice to
candy maker

1894
starts Hershey
Chocolate Company

Milton died in 1945. He is remembered for being a generous businessman. Today millions of people visit his town. His chocolate is still loved around the world.

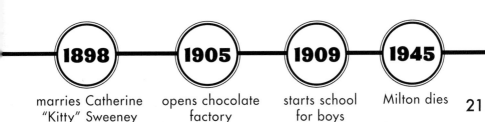

1898	1905	1909	1945
marries Catherine "Kitty" Sweeney	opens chocolate factory	starts school for boys	Milton dies

Glossary

apprentice—someone who learns a job or craft by working with a skilled person

energy—the strength to do active things without getting tired

generous—willing to share

invent—to think of and create something new; the new item is the invention

World War II—a war in which the United States, France, Great Britain, and other countries defeated Germany, Italy, and Japan

Critical Thinking Using the Common Core

1. Milton's company invented a chocolate bar that didn't melt in hot weather. What does invent mean? What do you think was important about this invention? What invention do you think would be important to create? (Integration of Knowledge and Ideas)

2. Describe what you see in the photo on page 16. Using clues from the photo and text, what do you think is happening in the photo? (Craft and Structure)

Read More

Malam, John. *Journey of a Bar of Chocolate.* Journey of a ... Chicago: Heinemann Library, 2013.

Mattern, Joanne. *Milton Hershey: Hershey's Chocolate Creator.* Checkerboard Biography Library. Edina, Minn.: ABDO Pub. Co., 2011.

Nelson, Robin. *From Cocoa Bean to Chocolate.* Food. Minneapolis: Lerner Publications Company, 2013.

Internet Sites

FactHound offers a safe, fun way to find Internet sites related to this book. All of the sites on FactHound have been researched by our staff.

Here's all you do:

Visit *www.facthound.com*

Type in this code: 9781476596402

Check out projects, games and lots more at
www.capstonekids.com

Index

Word Count: 271
Grade: 1
Early-Intervention Level: 22

Editorial Credits
Michelle Hasselius, editor; Lori Bye, designer; Tracy Cummins, media researcher;
Jennifer Walker, production specialist

Photo Credits
Capstone Press: Karon Dubuke, 1, 18; Corbis: Bettmann, cover, 20;
Courtesy of Hershey Community Archives: Hershey PA, 14; Milton Hershey School: 4, 6, 8,
12, 16; Shutterstock: Nomad Soul, cover background; Wikimedia: smallbones, 10